EASY ICE CREAM

RECIPES

TOP 10 RECIPES YOUR KIDS WILL LOVE

Bonus Recipes Included

BY R.L.WILLIAMS

Illustrations by Devin Mauldin

NEXLEV PUBLISHING

Nexlev Publishing, USA
Illustrations by Devin Mauldin
Printed in the United States of America

ACKNOWLEDGEMENTS

I want to thank the many people who contributed to the successful completion of this book---with special thanks to several key individuals:

My Aunt Bessie and Aunt Rosa, may they rest in peace, who taught me the importance of making your own meals and wrapping it up with a scrumptious dessert at the end. Summer Sunday dinners with these two sisters, a couple members from the local congregation, a triple scoop of Neapolitan Ice Cream, and a slice of homemade 7-Up Pound Cake were the best!

•

My "older-younger" sister, Erne, for her strength and inherently protective nature, knowing just what to say and do to help create an environment of continuous stability and success, and for being a sounding board for years of ideas and ventures.

•

My BFF, Marcie and Cousin Tammy, for being significantly invested in my success and for being available day or night to discuss book ideas and cover drafts. Your positive words have always kept me going.

•

Dave G., for inspiring me with your leadership, mentoring, public speaking success, volunteering for proofreading, and for being a listening ear for my publishing goals.

•

Mia A., for driving the distance when I needed it most, for your attention to detail, listening to ideas, offering suggestions, and non-stop encouragement.

•

My GS, Sandy L, for the many Power-chats, motivation, and strength. I'm inspired by your ambition. Thank you for regularly hearing ideas and reaching out to help.

•

Cecil Sr., for believing in me and reminding me when it's time for a much needed break.

•

Terrance M., for being an inspiring example of entrepreneurial success and for reminding me of the importance of creating "multiple streams of income."

•

A Very Special Thanks to Devin *(my personal motivation), for your creative illustrations, commitment to your artwork, our brainstorming sessions, unknowingly pushing me to greater heights, and for being key in creating a stress-free environment that allows me to flourish.*

Finally, an enormous thank you, to those who think you can't--- you absolutely can!

Table of Contents

Acknowlegements

Introduction

Chapter 1: We All Scream for Vanilla Ice Cream! *(No Ice Cream Maker Required)*

Chapter 2: Real Strawberries Ice Cream

Chapter 3: Chocolates Are a Girl's Best Friend

Chapter 4: Auntie's Banana Pudding Ice Cream *(No Ice Cream Maker Required)*

Chapter 5: Lemon Key Lime Ice Cream

Chapter 6: Peanut Ice Cream

Chapter 7: Green Ice Cream

Chapter 8: Berry Berry Good Ice Cream

Chapter 9: My Friend, Orangelo Ice Cream

Chapter 10: Fresh Strawberry Cheesecake Ice Cream

Chapter 11: Bonus Recipe #1: Cookies and Cream Dream Ice Cream

Bonus Recipe #2: Irish Brown Bread Ice Cream with Butterscotch

Bonus Recipe #3: Apple Crumble with Calvados and Crème Fraiche Ice Cream

Conclusion

Introduction

I want to thank you for choosing this book, 'EASY ICE CREAM RECIPES - TOP 10 RECIPES YOUR KIDS WILL LOVE!

If I were to tell you to find someone who doesn't like ice cream, it would definitely leave you searching for a long time. You will hardly find anyone who doesn't love a chilled and creamy bowl or cone of delicious ice cream. It is not just a favorite dessert of young and old alike, it is also one of the most booming industries around the world. But that is the problem, though it is such a beloved delicacy, most people end up buying tubs of ice cream from local supermarkets or ice cream parlors. Few take the time to make these delicious bursts of flavors at home.

The fact is making ice cream is not a difficult task. Rather, it is as fun and therapeutic as baking or cooking is. The best part is homemade ice cream is much healthier as compared to fatty and preservative-laden store brought products. You can incorporate as many different fresh fruit, crunchy nuts, and pretty much any other ingredient you fancy, and whip them into any ice cream mix of your choice.

I can't tell you how happy I am to present you with a book that takes me right down the memory lane. Back then, when I was a bit younger, sure we loved the neighborhood grocery store ice creams. But there was nothing better than churning our own quart of ice cold deliciousness. Besides in my family, the grown-ups would whip up the most perfect ice cream for dessert and would leave us craving for more. If my brother or I ever had a bad day, a bowl of mouth-watering ice cream would magically make our worries disappear.

I have to confess, most of the recipes mentioned in this book are a developed version of my family's original recipes. After all, how could their culinary skills not rub off on me after having spent so much of my time in the kitchen. I was one of those rare kids who loved to experiment with food. My love for food in those early years compelled me to come up with this special recipe book. And what could be more fascinating than ice cream recipes for kids!

There are about 13 interesting ice cream recipes in this book, which are extremely easy to make. I have tried to use the most readily available ingredients from the market to make these ice creams. The recipes used in this guide are pretty detailed including an ingredients list, step-by-step instructions, and a peppy introduction to each one of them. Even though the ice cream recipes are meant for kids, I have tried to be as innovative as possible, with the hope that folks of all ages will love them. You are also free to tweak the ingredients to your liking and come up with new flavors.

Nowadays anything basic isn't enough to catch most kid's attention. So, I promise you the recipes in this book are so different and lip-smacking that it will leave your kids no room to complain. Here's sincerely hoping that you will have fun reading this book as much as I have enjoyed writing it. Happy reading!

Chapter 1: We All Scream for Vanilla Ice Cream!
(No Ice Cream Maker Required)

Let's start with a hometown favorite everyone is sure to love. That's vanilla ice cream! Most will agree, a bowl or a cone of the ever-popular, good old vanilla ice cream will add a smile to any child's face! This crowd-pleaser takes me back to childhood memories growing up in the South during the blistering heat of the summer months.

Ingredients
- 1 14oz can Eagle Brand Sweetened Condensed Milk (cold)
- 2 cups heavy whipping cream (cold)
- 1 tsp. vanilla extract
- ¼ tsp. sea salt

Instructions
1. Pour 2 cups refrigerated heavy whipping cream into a large mixing bowl.
2. Using a hand mixer beat until the whipping cream becomes stiff.
3. Fold in half contents (approximately 7 oz.) of the sweetened condensed milk into the whipping cream and continue to beat.
4. Add the remaining sweetened condensed milk into the whipping cream mixture, along with the ¼ tsp. sea salt. Continue to mix.
5. Lastly, add the 1 tsp. vanilla extract and beat until the desired consistent is reached.
6. Place the vanilla ice cream mixture into a ½ gallon sealed container or larger and refrigerator 6-8 hours.

Serve: After the ice cream has been frozen for 6-8 hours, remove and serve with your favorite topics or eat alone.

Yields: Approx. 16 – 4 oz. servings (½ gallon of delicious ice cream)

Optional recipe suggestion:
Add 3 tablespoons of melted butter for a richer, creamier taste.

Chapter 2: Real Strawberries Ice Cream

Summer time calls for fresh fruit and fun. Kids of all ages will love this mouthwatering, cold treat! Ice cream gives the feel of summer, and strawberry ice cream is one that kids will want any day. This ice cream is as good as it gets! You can throw in some cake if you want to, since who does not like cake? Also, this ice cream is so pretty in pink, just like Molly Ringwald in 'The Facts of Life.' You cannot blame your kid if he or she cannot resist this ice cream. This ice cream is made using an ice cream maker and fresh strawberries and is worth the investment. Let's take a look at what makes this ice cream the best there is!

Ingredients
- ¾ cup heavy cream
- ½ cup granulated sugar
- ¼ teaspoon vanilla extract
- ¾ cup whole milk
- 2 large egg yolks
- 1 pint strawberries (about 1 ½ cups)

Instructions
1. Hull the strawberries. Chop the strawberries into chunks.
2. To make an ice bath: Half fill a bowl with water and ice. Place it aside.
3. Pour milk and cream into a saucepan. Add 1/3-cup sugar and stir.
4. Place the saucepan over low to medium heat.
5. When it begins to simmer, turn off the heat. Stir occasionally until sugar dissolves completely.

6. While the milk mixture is on heat, add egg yolks into a bowl and beat until it turns pale yellow.
7. Add about a cup of the milk mixture into the bowl of yolks. Whisk constantly while adding.
8. Pour the egg mix in a pan and place it back over low to medium heat.
9. Stir continuously with a heatproof spatula and cook until the mixture thickens and coats the spatula.
10. Take it off heat. Pass the mixture through a fine mesh strainer, placed over a bowl. Add vanilla and whisk until well combined.
11. Place the bowl in the prepared ice bath for 10-15 minutes.
12. Meanwhile, add strawberries and remaining sugar into a bowl. Toss well and let it sit at room temperature for 10-15 minutes. Mash the strawberries using a potato masher until the strawberries are small bits of the size of a pea.
13. Remove from ice bath when the mixture is cold.
14. Add mashed strawberries into it and stir. Keep the bowl covered with a plastic wrap. Press the plastic wrap lightly so that it touches the surface of the custard. Let it freeze in the fridge for at least 3-4 hours or overnight.
15. Pour into the ice cream maker and let it churn the ice cream as per the manufacturer's instructions manual.
16. Alternately, pour the mixture into an ice cream container and allow it to freeze. After about an hour of freezing, remove the ice cream from the freezer and whisk well. Refreeze and beat again after 30-40 minutes.
17. Repeat the above steps a couple of times more until well frozen without ice crystals.

18. The ice cream can last for 10 days.

Serve: After the ice cream has been frozen for 6-8 hours, remove and serve with your favorite toppings if desired or eat as it is.

Yields: Approx. 4 to 5 – 4 oz. servings

Chapter 3: Chocolates Are a Girl's Best Friend

Chocolate ice cream has an allure that is contrasting and every kid in the world loves it---well, many do. But, it is not only for the kids, adults will love this ice cream too. This was my cousin's favorite and to this day – she is a glutton for chocolate ice cream. This ice cream is made from cocoa and has a dark roasted flavor. Chocolate ice cream is cool, creamy, rich, and will leave you oh so happy!

This ice cream recipe is for those who are die-hard lovers of chocolate. This sweet, salty, bitter ice cream will blow your kid's mind. He or she will keep wanting more, so you may need to make an extra batch in case you run out of the first batch too quickly. This kind of ice cream has the right balance of milk and chocolate. Your kids may have tasted several chocolate ice creams before, but I am sure they will find that this is one of the best ice creams they have ever scooped into a cone. It does not take very long to make this ice cream and is easy to scoop out since it does not freeze immediately.

Ingredients
- 2/3 cup cocoa powder, unsweetened
- 2 cups milk or half and half
- 12 large yolks
- 3 teaspoons vanilla extract
- 4 cups heavy whipping cream
- 1 ½ cups sugar
- A pinch salt

Variations for chocolate chip or Choco-nut ice cream:
- *Chocolate chips, as required*
- *Nuts, chopped, as required*

Instructions

1. To make an ice bath: Half fill a bowl with water and ice. Place it aside.
2. Add yolks and salt into a bowl. Whisk until pale in color. Place it aside.
3. Place a medium saucepan over low to medium heat. Pour cream and milk. Add cocoa and sugar.
4. Warm the mixture until sugar dissolves, stirring constantly. Turn off the heat.
5. Add about a cup of this mixture into the bowl of yolk mixture whisking simultaneously.
6. Pour the egg mixture back into the saucepan.
7. Place the saucepan back over low to medium heat. Stir continuously with a heatproof spatula and cook until the mixture thickens and coats the spatula.
8. Take it off heat. Pass the mixture through a fine mesh strainer, placed over a bowl. Add vanilla and whisk until well combined.
9. Place the bowl in the prepared ice bath. Take it out from ice bath and keep the bowl covered with a plastic wrap. Press the plastic wrap lightly so that it touches the surface of the custard. Chill in the refrigerator for at least 3-4 hours or overnight.
10. Pour into the ice cream maker and let it churn the ice cream as per the manufacturer's instructions manual.
11. Alternately, pour the mixture into an ice cream container and allow it to freeze. After about an hour of freezing, remove the ice cream from the freezer and whisk well. Refreeze and beat again after 30-40 minutes.
12. Repeat the above steps a couple of times more until well frozen without ice crystals.
13. To make chocolate chip or Choco-nut ice cream:

14. Chocolate chips or nuts: To be added when the ice cream is semi- frozen. Stir well and freeze.

Serve: After the ice cream has been frozen for 6-8 hours, remove and serve.

Yields: Approx. 16-20 – 4 oz. servings

Chapter 4: Auntie's Banana Pudding Ice Cream
(No Ice Cream Maker Required)

Banana Pudding ice cream – that sounds like a dish anyone would definitely like, doesn't it? This is my personal favorite and I've found there are even a few restaurants and BBQ joints that serve a similar version of this ice cream. Your teens will definitely want to post this on their social media accounts after trying this banana pudding ice cream for the first time. This is made without using an ice cream maker and is very simple. The recipe is a Philadelphia style recipe, in the sense that you will not need to make custard using the eggs. All you need is cold whipped cream and milk! To give the ice cream the banana flavor, we will be using real bananas. People often dislike using whipped cream when they make ice cream, but we are using it in this recipe to give the ice cream a perfect texture when it is frozen. This ice cream is perfect for the little ones.

Ingredients
- 6 cups heavy whipping cream (cold)
- 2 teaspoons pure vanilla extract
- 1 banana, peeled, thinly sliced
- 1 banana, peeled, mashed
- 2 cups sweetened condensed milk
- ½ cup vanilla pudding mix
- 1 ½ cups crushed vanilla wafers
- Optionally, add a pack of banana smoothie mix for a richer taste

Instructions
1. Add heavy whipping cream and condensed milk into a stand mixer bowl.

2. Fix the whisk attachment to the mixer. Beat until it forms stiff peaks (2–3 minutes).
3. Beat in the pudding mix and mashed banana. Beat until well combined.
4. Add most of the sliced banana and vanilla wafers and fold using a silicone spatula.
5. Transfer into a loaf pan.
6. Decorate with remaining vanilla wafers and banana slices.
7. Place the loaf pan in the freezer until firm.

Serve: After the ice cream has been frozen for 5-8 hours, remove and serve.

Yields: Approx. 16-20 – 4 oz. servings

Chapter 5: Lemon Key Lime Ice Cream

Let me tell you a little about this ice cream. This is one flavor that you and your kids will wish was sold in stores, but it does not matter anymore since you can make this at home and it is extremely easy to make. It is a smooth, tangy ice cream that tastes just like the key lime pie. The lovely part of the ice cream is the lemon zest, which gives you the hint of sourness when you bite into it. If your kids like cookies and cream types of desserts over chocolate and vanilla flavored desserts, you should definitely try this at home. Your kids will feel like they are in heaven when they eat this ice cream during summer. You do not necessarily have to make this ice cream in summer. It is a flavor that can be eaten during any season or whenever you or your kids get the urge for a slice of fresh Key Lime Pie.

Ingredients

- 1 ¾ cups + 2 tablespoons white sugar
- 1 ½ tablespoons lemon zest, grated
- 1 cup + 2 tablespoons lime juice
- 3 large eggs
- 6 egg yolks
- 3 1/3 cups half and half cream

Instructions

1. To make an ice bath: Half fill a bowl with water and ice. Place it aside.
2. Add eggs, yolks, lemon zest, lime juice and sugar into a saucepan. Whisk until well combined.
3. Place the saucepan over low to medium heat. Stir continuously with a heatproof spatula and cook until the mixture thickens and coats the spatula.

4. Take it off heat. Pass the mixture through a fine mesh strainer, placed over a bowl.
5. Place the bowl in the prepared ice bath. Take it out from ice bath and keep the bowl covered with a plastic wrap. Press the plastic wrap lightly so that it touches the surface of the custard Chill in the refrigerator for at least 3-4 hours or overnight.
6. Pour into the ice cream maker and let it churn the ice cream as per the manufacturer's guidelines manual.
7. Transfer into a freezer safe container with a tight fitting lid. Freeze for 2 hours.
8. Alternately, pour the mixture into a freezer safe container and let it freeze. After about an hour of freezing, remove the ice cream from the freezer and whisk well. Refreeze and beat again after 30-40 minutes.
9. Repeat the above steps a couple of times more until well frozen without ice crystals.

Serve: After the ice cream has been frozen for 2 hours, remove and serve.

Yields: Approx. 16-20 – 4 oz. servings

Chapter 6: Peanut Butter Ice Cream

This ice cream is a dream come true for every peanut butter lover. If your kid loves peanut butter, you will have to make this ice cream every other day to satisfy their demands. This salty, sweet and creamy combination is one that is often served with pecan pies in restaurants and if your kids were to eat this, they would fall in love with it immediately. This recipe puts a new spin on one of my afterschool favorites--- peanut butter cookies---your kids are sure to love! This recipe will not fall short on expectations and will be one of the best ice creams you have ever sunken your spoon into.

Ingredients

- 2 cans (14 ounces each) sweetened condensed milk
- 2 ½ cups whole milk
- 2 cans (12 ounces each) evaporated milk
- 1 cup peanut butter, plain, unsweetened, unsalted, softened
- 4 teaspoons vanilla extract
- ½ cup white sugar
- 12 peanut butter cups, chopped

Instructions

1. Add evaporated milk, condensed milk and whole milk into a bowl. Mix until well combined.
2. Add peanut butter, vanilla and sugar and whisk until the sugar gets dissolved completely.
3. Keep the bowl covered with a plastic wrap. Press the plastic wrap lightly so that it touches the surface of the custard Chill in the refrigerator for at least 3-4 hours or overnight.

4. Pour into the ice cream maker and let it churn the ice cream as per the manufacturer's instructions manual.
5. When it reaches the semi- soft consistency, add peanut butter cups.
6. Transfer into a freezer safe container. Wrap the container with plastic wrap.
7. Place container in the freezer.
8. Alternately, pour the mixture into an ice cream container and allow it to freeze. After about an hour of freezing, remove the ice cream from the freezer and whisk well. Refreeze and beat again after 30-40 minutes.
9. Repeat the above steps a couple of times more until well frozen without ice crystals.
10. Add peanut butter cups when you whisk for the last time.

Serve: After the ice cream has been frozen for 2 hours, remove and serve.

Yields: Approx. 20 – 4 oz. servings

Chapter 7: Green Ice Cream

People all over the world have heard of Matcha Green Tea. You may have also had your first taste of Matcha Green tea when you took your first sip of the Starbucks Green Tea Frappuccino. This is a beverage that is available in most Japanese restaurants and has been used to prepare a variety of dishes.

Matcha is a type of green tea that is made by crushing green tea leaves. This is pretty bright in color and adds the green to the ice cream. It is a flavor that is popular for many reasons and its distinct grassy flavor makes this ice cream a favorite for most people.

This ice cream may not be something your kids will take a liking to immediately, but it is important to let them know that this ice cream will give them enough energy to run around the house or play all day long. You can eat this ice cream instead of drinking coffee in the morning if you want to.

Ingredients
- 2 cups whole milk
- 1 ½ cups white sugar
- 2 tablespoons matcha green powder or more to taste
- 4 cups heavy whipping cream
- 4 eggs

Instructions
1. Add matcha powder into a bowl and whisk until it is free from lumps.
2. Add a little milk and whisk until well combined.

3. Add rest of the milk and whisk well. Pour into a saucepan. Add cream into the saucepan.
4. Place the saucepan over medium - low heat. Stir occasionally. Turn off the heat when warmed.
5. Add eggs and sugar into a bowl and whisk well.
6. Add ½ cup of the matcha mixture into the bowl of eggs and stir constantly until well combined.
7. Add remaining matcha mixture in the similar manner.
8. Add the entire contents back into the saucepan. Place saucepan over medium–low heat.
9. Stir constantly until it is heated. Turn off the heat and let it cool completely.
10. Keep the bowl covered with a plastic wrap. Press the plastic wrap lightly so that it touches the surface of the custard. Let it freeze in the refrigerator for at least 3-4 hours or overnight.
11. Pour into the ice cream maker and let it churn the ice cream as per the manufacturer's instructions manual.
12. Transfer into a freezer safe container. Wrap the container with plastic wrap.
13. Place container in the freezer.
14. Alternately, pour the mixture into an ice cream container and allow it to freeze. After about an hour of freezing, remove the ice cream from the freezer and whisk well. Refreeze and beat again after 30-40 minutes.
15. Repeat the above steps a couple of times more until well frozen without ice crystals.

Serve: After the ice cream has been frozen for 2 hours, remove and serve.

Yields: Approx. 16 – 4 oz. servings

Optional: May substitute matcha for pistachio flavored jello.

Chapter 8: Berry Berry Good Ice Cream

So the weekend is around the corner and I'll guess you might be ready for some fun or even a relaxing weekend. Maybe there's even a party on the horizon or simply ready to dig in to some Berry delicious food. Well, just in case you forgot about the dessert or were too busy planning on your days off, I have just what you might need.

Summer time calls for some lip smacking berry ice cream, which will soothe your taste buds and leave you asking for more. Berry Berry Ice Cream can be a heavenly recipe for warmer months and instantly put you in the right mood. Berries are not only the healthiest of fruit, but they are loaded with anti-oxidants.

So, all you health conscious readers out there, you are simply going to fall in love with this recipe. Strawberries, blueberries, raspberries, take your pick or choose them all and make a delicious ice cream treat! There's a whole world of berries waiting for you to explore. When was the last time you enjoyed a creamy, berry ice cream? Think it's been too long? What are you waiting for? Let's get started.

Ingredients
- 1.1 pounds frozen mixed berries of your choice
- 24 ounces thickened cream
- 17.6 ounces caster sugar or super fine sugar
- 4 tablespoons lemon juice
- 24 ounces milk
- 2 vanilla beans, split, scrape the seeds
- 10 egg yolks

Instructions

1. To make an ice bath: Half fill a bowl with water and ice. Place it aside.
2. Add frozen berries into a large microwave safe bowl and microwave on high for 40 seconds.
3. The berries should not cook; they only have to be soft.
4. Add the berries into the food processor bowl and process until smooth.
5. Pass the berry mixture through a wire mesh strainer that is placed over a bowl. Do this in batches.
6. Discard the seeds and let it sit until you prepare the ice cream.
7. Add cream and milk into a saucepan. Add the vanilla bean seeds.
8. Place the saucepan over low to medium heat. When it begins to bubble, turn off the heat.
9. Add yolks and sugar into a bowl and whisk until it turns light yellow in color.
10. Whisk in about ½ cup of the milk mixture. Whisk constantly until well combined.
11. Add rest of the milk mixture whisking constantly while adding.
12. Clean the saucepan and add the entire mixture into the saucepan.
13. Place the saucepan over low heat. Stir continuously with a heatproof spatula and cook until the mixture thickens and coats the spatula.
14. Take it off heat. Pass the mixture through a fine mesh strainer, placed over a bowl.
15. Place the bowl in the prepared ice bath. Take it out from ice bath and add pureed berries and lemon juice.
16. Keep the bowl covered with a plastic wrap. Press the plastic wrap lightly so that it touches the surface of

the custard. Let it freeze in the fridge for at least 3-4 hours or overnight.

17. Pour into the ice cream maker and let it churn the ice cream as per the manufacturer's instructions manual.

18. Transfer into a freezer safe container with a tight fitting lid. Freeze for 4-5 hours.

19. Alternately, pour the mixture into an ice cream container and allow it to freeze. After about an hour of freezing, remove the ice cream from the freezer and whisk well. Refreeze and beat again after 30-40 minutes.

20. Repeat the above steps a couple of times more until well frozen without ice crystals.

Serve: After the ice cream has been frozen for 4-5 hours, remove and serve.

Yields: Approx. 16-20 – 4 oz. servings

Chapter 9: My Friend, Orangelo Ice Cream

Ever heard of Orangelo ice cream? You think it sounds bizarre? Well, that's because we aren't doing anything normal here, my loves. This ice cream is as bright as the color of Orangelo and is sure to send your taste buds into a frenzy. Don't believe me? Try this super awesome Orangelo ice cream that sure to add some color to your life. Orangelo, the Puerto-Rican hybrid citrus food gives the ice cream a mild flavor of grapefruit as well as orange. If you are tired of eating those dark chocolaty flavored ice creams, some Orangelo ice cream might just be what you need. I love experimenting with different flavors when it comes to ice cream. So when I first created this recipe, my aim was to come up with a mild flavored, wildly refreshing ice cream. Tell you a secret---I love orangelos! So much that during the first couple of attempts, I ended up eating all of them instead of making ice cream. But on a serious note, this is one of my favorite recipes and I insist that you try it out.

Ingredients
- 3 packages (6 ounces each) orange Jell-O
- 3 cans mandarin oranges along with its juice
- 3 cups soft vanilla ice cream
- 2 bananas, peeled, sliced
- 1 cup crushed pineapple
- 3 cups hot water

Instructions
1. Add Jell-O into a mixing bowl. Pour boiling water and stir.
2. Add vanilla ice cream and whisk with a wire whisk until well combined.

3. Add mandarin juice and whisk well.
4. Place banana slices, crushed pineapple and mandarin oranges into individual serving bowls.
5. Pour the Jell-O mixture into the bowls.
6. Chill in the refrigerator until set.

Serve: After the dessert has been set for 1-2 hours, remove and serve.

Yields: Approx. 20 -25 – 4 oz. servings

Chapter 10: Fresh Strawberry Cheesecake Ice Cream *(No Ice Cream Maker Required)*

The very thought of strawberry cheesecake ice cream sounds like a double treat. I mean cheesecake and strawberries---in ice cream. Whoaaa! How cool is that! This creamy recipe is bursting with an extremely fruity, tangy and sweet flavor. It will almost taste like the best strawberry cheesecake ever has been turned into a heavenly bowl of ice cream.

I was always a big cheesecake fan (I am a fan of literally all ice-creams, but believe me when I say this, this one's very close to my heart). There's truly nothing like a homemade ice cream that combines the goodness of strawberries with a richly textured cream cheese---unless you aren't big on cream cheese. In that case, we have other recipes for you.

For now, let's focus on this super-delicious dessert that is easy to make and sure to make your guests really happy. This super easy recipe is eggless and doesn't require churning. When I was made this ice cream for the first time, I instantly knew that this flavor would stand out. Let's see how this turns out.

Ingredients

- 2 packages (8 ounces each) cream cheese, at room temperature
- 2 cans (14 ounces each) sweetened condensed milk
- 3 cups fresh strawberries, chopped into small pieces
- ¼ cup sugar, powdered
- 4 teaspoon lemon zest or 1 teaspoon lemon extract
- ½ cup whipping cream (cool whip)
- 6 squares of graham crackers or 24 vanilla wafers, crumbled

Instructions

1. Add cream cheese, lemon zest, condensed milk and whipping cream into a bowl. Whisk until well combined.
2. Transfer into a freezer safe container with a tight fitting lid. Place in the freezer until semi solid.
3. Remove from the freezer and beat with an electric mixer until smooth and creamy. Add the strawberries and sugar powder and stir.
4. Stir in the crumbled graham crackers. Transfer into freezer safe container and allow it to freeze until firm.
5. Remove from the freezer and let it sit at room temperature for 10 minutes before serving.
6. Scoop and serve.

Serve: After the ice cream has been frozen for 4-5 hours, remove and serve.

Yields: Approx. 16 – 4 oz. servings

Chapter 11: Bonus Recipe #1 - Cookies and Cream Dream Ice Cream

Cookies and cream, does that just sound perfect? It's one of the most classic combinations that are popular across the globe. Almost anyone who loves cookies will absolutely love this ice cream. Creamier and richer than most store-bought ice creams, this version is quite easy to put together. With a combination like this, you will never fail to impress your loved ones. And it's extremely easy too. No fancy ingredients, no fussy equipment, just a whole lot of love. Out of cookies? No problem. You can also use Oreo crumbles instead of actual cookies to make this ice cream. It's pretty fuss-free and takes less than an hour to make. The only difficult part is waiting for the ice cream to freeze. This highly indulgent ice cream is every chocolate lover's favorite. You just can't wait for it to melt in your mouth. Let's not waste any more time. Here it is...

Ingredients
- 6 cups heavy cream
- 1 ½ cups sugar
- 1 teaspoon kosher salt
- 8 ounces chocolate wafer cookies or any other sandwich cookies like Oreo cookies
- 2 cups whole milk
- 2 teaspoons pure vanilla extract
- 10 large egg yolks

Instructions
1. To make an ice bath: Half fill a bowl with water and ice. Place it aside.
2. Pour milk and cream into a saucepan. Add salt, vanilla, sugar and stir.
3. Place the saucepan over low to medium heat. Stir occasionally until sugar dissolves completely.

4. When it begins to simmer, turn off the heat.
5. Add egg yolks into a bowl and beat until it turns pale yellow.
6. Add about a cup of the milk mixture into the bowl of yolks. Whisk constantly while adding.
7. Pour the egg mixture into the saucepan. Place the saucepan back over low heat.
8. Stir continuously with a heatproof spatula and cook until the mixture thickens and coats the spatula.
9. Take it off heat. Pass the mixture through a fine mesh strainer, placed over a bowl.
10. Place the bowl in the prepared ice bath for 10-15 minutes. Remove from ice bath and keep the bowl covered with a plastic wrap. Press the plastic wrap lightly so that it touches the surface of the custard. Let it freeze in the fridge for at least 3-4 hours or overnight.
11. Pour into the ice cream maker and let it churn the ice cream as per the manufacturer's instructions manual.
12. Add the cookies into a plastic re-sealable bag. Crush the cookies lightly with a rolling pin.
13. Pour ice cream into a freezer safe container. Sprinkle cookies over it. Stir until the cookie pieces are well distributed in the ice cream. Cover the container with plastic wrap and freeze.
14. Alternately, pour the mixture into an ice cream container and allow it to freeze. After about an hour of freezing, remove the ice cream from the freezer and whisk well. Refreeze and beat again after 30-40 minutes.
15. Repeat the above steps a couple of times more until well frozen without ice crystals. Add the cookies after beating for the last time.

16. Stir until the cookie pieces are well distributed. Cover the container with plastic wrap and freeze

Serve: After the ice cream has been frozen for 2-3 hours, remove and serve.

Yields: Approx. 16 – 4 oz. servings

Chapter 12: Bonus Recipe #2 - Irish Brown Bread Ice Cream with Butterscotch

So you have got some Irish brown bread leftover from last night and don't know what to do with it? No, slathering thick slices of butter on it isn't exactly going to turn into a tasty treat. But here's a fantastic idea. How about if you make some ice cream out of it? I am so glad that I stumbled upon this recipe at a friend's on St. Patrick's Day celebration many years ago. This extremely flavorful ice cream is one of the most brilliant inventions in the world of ice creams. You may rarely come across anyone who knows how to make this ice cream here in the US, but apparently, it's pretty common in Ireland. Some even call it the "grape nut ice cream" and it's totally mesmerizing. This could be the most spot on description for an ice cream that is made out of brown sugar, which lends a caramelized depth and is loaded with cream cheese. The cream cheese also gives it the correct amount of tanginess, which goes well with the sweetness of some cinnamon-y brown bread. I wish I could say that you can nail this ice cream without any hiccups if you are a first-timer. But as long as you follow this recipe step by step right from the get-go, you will face fewer troubles.

Ingredients
For Irish brown bread:
- 1 ½ cups all-purpose flour + extra to dust the pan
- 1 ½ teaspoons kosher salt
- ¾ cup wheat bran
- ½ cup steel cut oats
- 1 ¾ cups whole wheat flour
- ½ cup wheat germ
- 2 teaspoons baking soda
- 2 cups buttermilk

- 2 tablespoons dark brown sugar
- 3 teaspoons sunflower or vegetable oil
- Unsalted butter, to grease

For ice cream:
- 2 cups full fat milk
- 1 cup + 2 tablespoons sugar
- 4 ¼ cups heavy cream
- 10 cups stale Irish brown bread – crumble it finely
- 2 vanilla beans, halved lengthwise
- 8 large egg yolks
- ½ cup + 2 tablespoons packed dark brown sugar

For butterscotch:
- ½ cup salted butter
- 1 teaspoon vanilla extract
- 2 ½ cups heavy cream
- 2 cups dark brown sugar
- 2 teaspoons kosher salt

Instructions
To make bread –

1. Grease a large loaf pan with a little butter. Sprinkle flour lightly on the buttered area. Set aside.
2. Sift together all-purpose flour, salt and baking soda into a bowl. Stir in whole wheat flour, wheat germ, wheat bran, ¼ cup oats and brown sugar.
3. Make a well in the center of the mixture. Add buttermilk and oil in the center.
4. Mix until well combined and a dough is formed. Make sure that you do not knead or over mix it.
5. Place the dough into the prepared loaf pan. Sprinkle ¼ cup oats on top and press lightly on to the dough.

6. Bake in a preheated oven at 375° for about 45 minutes or a toothpick when inserted in the center is clean when removed.
7. Let the bread cool in the pan for 5-7 minutes. Take out the bread from the loaf pan and place on a wire rack. Let it cool completely.
8. It is preferable to make the bread a couple of days in advance.
9. To make an ice bath: Half fill a bowl with water and ice. Place it aside.

To make ice cream –

1. Add milk into a saucepan. Add the vanilla bean seeds.
2. Place the saucepan over low to medium heat. When it begins to bubble, turn off the heat. Stir constantly for a couple of minutes.
3. Remove the vanilla bean halves and discard it.
4. Add yolks and sugar into a bowl and whisk until it turns light yellow in color.
5. Whisk in the milk in a thin stream. Whisk constantly until just combined. Pour the egg mixture in a pan
6. Place the pan over low heat. Stir continuously with a heatproof spatula and cook until the mixture thickens and coats the spatula.
7. Take it off heat. Pass the mixture through a fine mesh strainer, placed over a bowl.
8. Place the bowl in the prepared ice bath. Add cream and stir until well combined. Remove from ice bath when cooled completely.
9. Pour into the ice cream maker and let it churn the ice cream as per the manufacturer's instructions manual.

10. Meanwhile, add brown sugar and 2 tablespoons water into a large saucepan. Place the saucepan over low to medium heat.
11. Heat until sugar dissolves completely. Add breadcrumbs and stir until well combined. Take it off heat and set aside to cool.
12. When the ice cream is of soft serve consistency, add the bread and stir well.
13. Transfer into a freezer safe container. Cover the container with a tight fitting lid or with plastic wrap. Place in the freezer until firm.

To make butterscotch –
1. Place a saucepan over low to medium heat. Add butter, sugar, cream and salt.
2. Stir constantly until the sugar dissolves completely. Turn off the heat and add vanilla. Mix until well combined.

Serve: After the ice cream has been frozen for 2-3 hours, remove and serve in bowls. Drizzle warm butterscotch sauce on top. Spoon some whipped cream on top if desired and serve.

Yields: Approx. 24 – 4 oz. servings

Chapter 13: Bonus Recipe #3 – Apple Crumble with Calvados and Crème Fraiche Ice Cream

Raise your hands if you like apple crumble!! I love apple crumble. Now would you like some apple crumble on your ice cream? It's almost like a work of art. It was my heartfelt wish to re-create the flavor of apple crumble in ice cream and I seemed to have nailed it with this recipe. Also, calvados has been used for bumping up the apple flavor, but if you don't have it handy, you can also use some brandy. Let's go!

Ingredients

For crumble:

- 1 1/3 cups all-purpose flour
- 2 teaspoons baking powder
- ½ teaspoon freshly grated nutmeg
- ¾ cup sugar
- ½ teaspoon kosher salt
- 1 ½ cups unsalted butter, melted, cooled

For apples:

- 4 medium apples like Granny Smith apples, cut into ¼ inch pieces
- 1 teaspoon pure vanilla extract
- ¼ teaspoon kosher salt
- 4 tablespoons calvados or any other brandy
- ½ cup sugar
- ¼ teaspoon ground cinnamon
- ¼ teaspoon freshly ground pink peppercorns

For ice cream:

- 3 cups whole milk
- ½ teaspoon kosher salt
- 4 cups crème fraiche

- 1 ¼ cups sugar
- 12 large egg yolks
- 1 teaspoon pure vanilla extract

Instructions

1. Place a sheet of parchment paper on a rimmed baking sheet. Set aside.
2. Add flour, baking powder, sugar, nutmeg and salt into a bowl and stir. Add butter and mix with a fork until it is of the texture of moist sand.
3. Place in the refrigerator for 20-30 minutes or until cold.
4. Spread the crumble on the rimmed baking sheet.
5. Place rack in the center of the oven. Place the baking sheet in the oven.
6. Bake in a preheated oven at 350° for about 15 minutes. Place baking sheet on a wire rack. When it cools, break into smaller pieces.

To make apples –

1. Add apples, vanilla, salt, pink peppercorns, sugar and cinnamon into a saucepan and stir. Let it rest for 30 minutes to macerate.
2. Cook the apple mixture over low heat until apples are slightly soft. Turn off the heat and cool for 5 minutes.
3. Add calvados and stir until well combined. Set aside to cool completely.

To make an ice bath –

1. Half fill a bowl with water and ice. Place it aside.

To make ice cream –

1. Add milk into a heatproof bowl. Add salt and a cup of sugar.

2. Place the heatproof bowl over a double boiler over medium - low heat. When the mixture begins to steam, remove bowl from the double boiler.
3. Stir until the sugar dissolves completely.
4. Add yolks and remaining sugar into a bowl and whisk until it turns light yellow in color.
5. Whisk in about ½ cup of milk in a thin stream. Whisk constantly until just combined. Pour the egg mixture into a heatproof bowl which.
6. Whisk until well combined.
7. Place the heatproof bowl back into the double boiler. Increase the heat to medium heat. Stir continuously with a heatproof spatula and cook until the mixture thickens and coats the spatula.
8. Take it off heat. Pass the mixture through a fine mesh strainer, placed over a bowl. Add crème fraiche and stir until well combined. If the mixture does not look thick anymore, place the bowl in the double boiler for some more time until thick.
9. Pass the mixture through a fine mesh strainer, placed over a bowl.
10. Place the bowl in the prepared ice bath. Add vanilla and stir. Remove from ice bath when cooled completely. Cover the bowl with plastic wrap and chill for 6–8 hours.
11. Pour into the ice cream maker and let it churn the ice cream as per the manufacturer's instructions manual.
12. When the ice cream is of soft serve consistency, add crumble and apples and churn for 30 seconds.
13. You can serve it right away if you like soft serve consistency.
14. Transfer into a freezer safe container with a tight fitting lid.

Serve: After the ice cream has been frozen for 2-3 hours remove and serve in bowls.

Yields: Approx. 16 – 4 oz. servings

Conclusion

On that sweet note, we have come to the end of this book. I want to thank you all once again for choosing this book and I sincerely hope that you have a fun time whipping and churning these recipes.

I have ensured that all the ingredients used in these recipes are easily available so you don't find yourself scouting for exotic ingredients. One trip to the grocery store is enough to stock all the ingredients of the recipes. Sometimes, it's not so easy to impress today's kids. They are always on the lookout for tastier and amusing food and sometimes the food they liked yesterday is not the food they like today. You parents know exactly what I mean. Like plain vanilla or strawberry just won't cut it!! This makes the competition among ice cream makers much fiercer.

The major problem we face with kids today is that almost everything they put in their mouth is store-bought. These packaged ice creams are loaded with preservatives and food colors, which are harmful for your kid's health in the long run. Instead, I urge you to try out these homemade ice creams that are not only tasty, but are made out of simple ingredients.

Like I said earlier, please feel free to add as many fresh fruits, nuts, or other ingredients to these existing recipes and come up with your new flavors and favorites. Try to use fresh and if possible organically grown ingredients for best result. If you are using nuts, make sure the nuts aren't stale and have a good crunch to them. Remember, the end result largely depends on the quality of the ingredients used.

So what are you waiting for? Get your ice cream makers out, put on that apron and let's get churning.

Made in the USA
Las Vegas, NV
15 December 2023

82945103R00028